20

COMMUNICATION

TIPS @

WORK

A Quick and Easy Guide to
Successful Business Relationships

ERIC MAISEL Ph.D.

NEW WORLD LIBRARY
NOVATO, CALIFORNIA

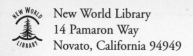
New World Library
14 Pamaron Way
Novato, California 94949

Front cover design by Mary Beth Salmon
Text design and typography by Tona Pearce Myers

Library of Congress Cataloging-in-Publication Data
Maisel, Eric, 1947–
    20 communication tips at work : a quick and easy guide to successful business relationships / Eric Maisel.
        p.   cm.
    ISBN 1-57731-128-0 (alk. paper)
    1. Business communication. 2. Communication in management. I. Title: Twenty communication tips at work. II. Title.
HF5718 .M348 2001
658.4'5—dc21   00-013266

First Printing, April 2001
ISBN 1-57731-128-0
Printed in Canada on acid-free, recycled paper
Distributed to the trade by Publishers Group West

10 9 8 7 6 5 4 3 2

FOR ANN, AGAIN

Contents

A few simple communication skills can make our experience at work (and at home) far more rewarding in every way, far more fulfilling. In his introduction, Eric Maisel says that with the principles in this little book you can "transform yourself into a workplace wizard." After working with Eric and with this fine book he has crafted, we have no doubt that he is not exaggerating.

Don't underestimate this book — it is simple, it is short, but it is also powerful. There's a kind of magic in it, and you can discover what it is by just flipping through and reading a few pages. We can almost guarantee that, within a day or two, you'll find yourself remembering something you read in this book. Even more important, you'll find yourself applying it in the workplace and changing the dynamics of your whole office, because you've changed your usual behavior into something far more effective.

You hold in your hands the tools to become a skilled communicator. It is a guidebook for wizards at work. The tools are not difficult to use, and the rewards are certainly worth the effort.

INTRODUCTION

Today's workplace is a dynamic, competitive, fast-paced, stressful, complex environment. Technological change happens overnight, corporations merge, divisions disappear, and products are old-fashioned the instant they appear. For all this twenty-first-century speed and flux, human communication has not changed since the dawn of time. A thousand years ago, people said things like "I can't enter the joust unless you get me that armor by Tuesday" and "Can I skip the knights' meeting and get on with my Holy Grail quest?" Today people say things like "I've got to have that report by noon" and "Can I duck the business meeting and get some actual work done?" The more things change, the more workplace communication remains the same.

I've been teaching working adults in a university management program for the past fifteen years and I've been a family therapist even longer. More times than I can count, I've seen people miss the opportunity to express what was on their minds, say one thing when they meant another, and overlook the importance of messages directed their way. They harmed themselves at work by what they said, by what they didn't say, or by what they failed to hear. They have also helped themselves by speaking directly when direct speech was called for, holding their tongues in situations that cried out for discretion, and unraveling the mixed messages they received. Success or failure at work often hinges on our expertise as speakers and listeners.

Many skills are valuable at work, but one

skill is essential: the ability to communicate. Whether you are presenting your ideas at a committee meeting, dashing off fifteen E-mails in a row, chatting with a coworker at the copy machine, evaluating an employee, or closing a deal over the phone, what you are doing is communicating. These exchanges are the backbone and the life blood of every organization and every relationship. Learn the principles of effective workplace communication contained in this little book and transform yourself into a workplace wizard!

20

COMMUNICATION

TIPS @

WORK

TIP 1

Never treat work
communications
cavalierly.

When you call your best friend to shoot the breeze, you can let down your hair and not worry about measuring every word you say. But when you are at work, all communications are meaningful and important. Every message you send provides information about you as a worker, a team player, a potential leader, or a potential problem. Every message you receive reveals aspects of your work environment and informs you about your fellow workers.

What you say goes a long way to determining how you are viewed. Measure your words and think before you speak. What you hear arms you with the knowledge you need to safeguard your livelihood. Remember to listen.

MESSAGES AT WORK ARE
ALWAYS SIGNIFICANT.
THEY REVEAL WHO YOU
ARE AND THEY EDUCATE
YOU ABOUT YOUR
FELLOW WORKERS.

TIP 2

Respond to messages at work in a calculated way.

At work we are bombarded by messages, from our coworkers, our boss, from other departments, from our customers, from everywhere. How much time can we spend on the two hundred E-mails we get each day, on the new safety regulations that just appeared in our in-box, or on that memo about a retirement party for someone whose name rings no bell?

Even if we only have a split second at our disposal to process each message, we still need to *calculate* our responses. First we need to understand the message. Are we being invited to the retirement party, being asked to part with $20 for a gift, or just being updated on some office news? Then we need to calculate how we want to respond by reading between the lines, reflecting on the sender's importance, deciding what would be politic to do, and so on. This may seem like a lot to do but we are excellent calculating machines and we can do all of this in no time flat, just as long as we *pay attention.* Quick as a wink we can decide whether to RSVP our acceptance, write a check, or crumple up the memo and toss it away.

The secret to calculating is *pausing.* Even if you only pause for a second or two, you give yourself time to think. If the conversation is live, rather than via E-mail or memo, and you need more than a second to think, you provide yourself with the pause you need by using language. You say something like "Let me think about that. I'll get back to you first thing this afternoon." Always give yourself the chance to make the right decision by taking a few seconds to gather your wits.

CALCULATE BEFORE YOU COMMUNICATE.

TIP 3

Get brilliant about
hidden agendas.

Every message has an intention. But often the sender's intention is hidden from view — on purpose.

If we work together and I say to you, "How are you feeling, Bob?" it's altogether likely that I have a calculated follow-up in mind. It might be something like "If you're over the flu, Bob, I need you to work over-time" or "If you're in a good mood, Bob, I'd like you to handle my calls when I leave early today." Many messages in the workplace are innocent but many are our coworkers' hidden agenda items. These you need to decode so that you can answer in the way that serves your purposes.

Remember: Having a hidden agenda isn't a vice. We all have them. What having a hidden agenda means is that a person wants what he or she wants. Still, you need to know *what* that agenda is and what *your* agenda is, too. Then you can answer smartly.

How can you tell what a coworker is really saying? Experience is the guide. When you deal with a person for awhile you get a sense of what her messages mean. The roles people play in an organization also affect the meaning of their messages. Get in the habit of testing every message in the following way:

1. What are the words?
2. Given the person and his or her role, what do the words probably mean?
3. Given their probable meaning, how do I want to reply?

Here are a few examples:

SITUATION A. When you intuit that a coworker wants to dump her work on you:

"How are you today, Bob?"

"Swamped!"

SITUATION B. When you intuit that your boss has some assignment to hand out and you want to indicate your availability:

"How are you today, Bob?"

"Terrific!"

SITUATION C. When you're not sure what a coworker wants and decide to keep your options open:

"How are you today, Bob?"

"Depends on what sort of day this becomes!"

REPLY TO THE MEANING IN A MESSAGE, NOT TO THE WORDS. THAT WAY YOU WILL ALWAYS MEAN WHAT YOU SAY.

FOUR TIPS FOR COMMUNICATING VIA E-MAIL

1. Think things through before you say them. You have the great luxury with E-mail of having time to think. You can draft your E-mail or your E-mail reply, read it through, and carefully consider what you are about to say. Don't send or reply until you are really ready! Just because E-mail messages move at the speed of light doesn't mean that you have to move that fast.

2. Take your doubts seriously. If there is something in the E-mail that you are about to send that troubles you, that makes you wonder if you are saying the right thing, or that in some other way sends up a warning flare,

take your doubts seriously. In most cases it is better to take the "offending" material out, even if you can't identify what the problem is or if there is a problem.

3. What you say is important, but how you say it is equally important. You want to cultivate a warm, nonjudgmental way of speaking that counterbalances the basic coldness of E-mail and that also serves your needs. The following are some circumlocutions you might want to cultivate:

- "I wonder if you might want to try...."
- "I was thinking that it might be useful if we...."
- "Do you think it might be a good idea if you called...."
- "I wonder if it would be wise for us to meet...."

- "I wanted to double-check some points with you, to make sure that I got them right...."

Send yourself some practice E-mail and rehearse this gentler, kinder way of communicating.

4. Don't overreact to the tone of the E-mail you receive. Many people send out E-mails that have a curt, blunt, cold, or aggressive edge, but very often they do not mean to be sending that message (of course, sometimes they do!). Take the tone of the E-mail you receive with several grains of salt and try not to get in a huff because the sender has left out the niceties of polite conversation.

TIP 4

If you can't decode an
important message,
ask for clarification.

Most people are poor communicators. The messages they send often leave us feeling uncertain about what was said. When that happens, we have three choices. We can try to interpret the message as best we can, act accordingly, and see if we made the right guess. We can ignore the message, hoping that it wasn't very important. Or we can go back to the sender and say, "I'm not sure I understood you. Can I tell you what I think I heard?"

If someone you work with regularly sends you messages that you don't understand, it isn't practical to ask for clarification every single time. You have to pick and choose. Most of the time you will make a valiant effort to interpret the message and get on with your business. Once in awhile you will ignore the message completely. Every so often an important message will come your way that you know you need to understand but just can't decode. Then you need to take a deep breath, prepare yourself, and ask for clarification.

In such situations, all of the following are reasonable gambits:

- "Dave, about that E-mail you just sent me. My mind is really foggy today. Can you go over that part about the 'multilevel restructuring package' again?"
- "Dave, I'm really excited to be working with you on the multilevel restructuring package! But I'm not altogether sure what it means. Could you explain it to me again?"
- "Dave, I was trying to make some notes on that restructuring package. But I got myself pretty confused. Can you tell me a little more about it?"

Often we have to guess at the meaning of a message, because it is impractical to ask for clarification every time some message confuses us. But when a message feels *important* and we really can't decode it, then asking for clarification is the only sensible choice.

REMEMBER — AN UNCLEAR
MESSAGE STAYS UNCLEAR,
UNTIL YOU GET CLARIFICATION
FROM THE PERSON WHO SENT IT.

TIP 5

When you want someone to understand you, be clear.

Clarity is like honesty. Sometimes it's easier to fib than to tell the truth and sometimes it's easier to dart and dodge than to say what's on your mind. You won't be clear in your communications unless you actually *want* to be clear. If you decide that you *do* want to be clear, then you need to identify precisely what you want to say and communicate that message in a simple, direct, uncluttered way.

UNCLEAR: "This outer office could use some art! Why don't you check into that?"

CLEAR: "I'd like you to go online this morning and see if you can find a Web site that sells African artifacts. I'm looking for carved stone figures from Zaire for the outer office. Just bookmark any sites you find and I'll come and take a look."

UNCLEAR: "I'd love to contribute to that report you're working on. So maybe I can give you some input later on and you can get it incorporated into the report? Now, don't feel pressured to use my ideas, but I've got a feeling you'll like them!"

CLEAR: "When you get to part five of that report you're preparing, I think you'll conclude that we can't have Christmas bonuses *and* a new computer network. But I have an idea how we can manage both. So when you get to that part, check in with me."

CLARITY IS A RESPONSIBILITY.
IF YOU AREN'T BEING CLEAR,
YOU'RE SHIRKING YOUR DUTY.

TIP 6

Know that you've been
heard by checking in
and asking questions.

Sometimes we're too tired to send a clear message. Sometimes we're too frazzled. Sometimes the person to whom we're talking isn't listening. Sometimes we think that we've sent a clear message but the group sitting around the table looks puzzled. Sometimes we have the feeling that the E-mail we just sent off to every department barely communicated our message.

Some of these are *sender* problems and some of these are *receiver* problems. But, in fact, they are all *our* problem. If we needed to get our message across and we didn't, then we have necessary repair work to do. We can accomplish this by taking the time — and mustering the courage — to check in and ask questions like these:

- "Betty, could you tell me what you think I was saying in my last E-mail? I'm not sure I was clear."

- "Harriet, I wanted to make sure that you got my message. Was I clear that I need the report *before* the meeting, not *after,* the way we usually do it? My memo may have been ambiguous."
- "I'm really tired and I'm not sure I'm saying this well. Could I get a little feedback from the group to make sure I'm articulating what's on my mind?"
- "George, you look puzzled. Did you have a question?"

This repair work takes courage. You may feel embarrassed and fear looking foolish when you admit that the message you sent might not have been clear. It also requires that you pay attention. You can't know that you should check in and ask questions if you haven't an intuition that something is wrong somewhere. If you're willing to pay attention and act courageously you can clear up these gaffes quickly and easily, just by reopening the lines of communication.

IF YOU THINK THAT YOUR
MESSAGE HASN'T BEEN HEARD —
IT PROBABLY HASN'T BEEN.

EIGHT STRATEGIES FOR HANDLING PERFORMANCE ANXIETY AT WORK

Maybe you have to give a presentation to your peers or in front of your bosses. Maybe you want to ask for a raise or to change your vacation schedule. Maybe you have to start training new employees. All of these are situations that engender anxiety, that special anxiety known as stage fright or performance anxiety. Anxiety can severely hamper a person's ability to communicate, so you will want to learn some strategies for dealing with performance anxiety at work. Here are eight strategies:

1. Rehearse and then rehearse some more. Nothing reduces performance anxiety

better than really knowing your material.

2. Accept that you are anxious. Just surrendering to the fact that you are anxious allows you to breathe a little easier.

3. Don't overdramatize your symptoms. Yes, you may have some butterflies or need to go to the bathroom, but that isn't the end of the world.

4. Make note cards and, if the situation permits, use them. It is better to have to look at a note card than to have no idea whatsoever what to say next.

5. Learn a calming guided visualization, meditation, or breathing exercise and use it before your performance.

6. Eat and drink lightly beforehand.

7. Surrender to the possibility that you may make mistakes and affirm that you will be okay even if you do.

8. Rehearse. Practice. Get ready. Then, when the curtain rises, smile!

TIP 7

Don't let your
nerves stop you
from delivering
your message.

Our fears get in the way of our ability to communicate. Sometimes we know what we're afraid of: that if we said what was on our mind we might open up a can of worms, cause an interpersonal rift, cast ourselves in a bad light, or let a secret out of the bag. More often, we can't articulate what we fear. A lot of the time we don't even know that fear and anxiety are present. Most of the time, though, you can be pretty sure that if you have an important message to send, one that may have repercussions, your nerves are going to get involved. They may even prevent you from speaking.

For this reason, you want to grow aware of what you're *not* saying at work. Have you said nothing about your workload doubling? Have you wanted to try your hand at a new challenge but not gotten around to asking your supervisor for permission? Is the person with whom you share your work space annoying you by allowing her friends from the third floor to drop by whenever they like?

You know that you should say something in each of these situations, but still you don't. Why? Because the fear that maybe you'll say the wrong thing and make matters worse is stopping you.

Your fear may be reasonable or it may be unreasonable. If it is reasonable, you may want to hold your tongue. If you don't really have much to fear and your nerves are just getting in the way, then have a quiet conversation with yourself and calm yourself down. Tell yourself that you needn't be frightened. Prepare what you want to say — and then say it.

FEAR CAN BE A GIFT —
OR A CURSE.
DON'T LET YOUR NERVES SILENCE
YOU UNNECESSARILY.

TIP 8

When warning
bells go off,
hold your tongue.

A moment ago I suggested that you shouldn't hold your tongue when you have an important message to deliver. Now I'd like to suggest that you *should* hold your tongue in a wide variety of situations: when you want to vent, when you hope to get a dig in, when you haven't thought through what you're about to say, when you get the urge to give an employee an off-the-cuff evaluation, when you're about to go back on your word, or when you feel like giving somebody a piece of your mind. Many situations at work require that we stop, think, and *refrain* from speaking.

Practically nothing make us more miserable and causes us more trouble than saying something that, an instant later, we wish we hadn't said and could take back. Not only do we risk harming our relationship with a customer, a coworker, one of our employees, or our boss, but we end up spending countless hours — even days and weeks — obsessing about why we were so foolish as to say that thing, dreaming up ways of patching up the rift, and calculating how badly we damaged the relationship. We have less mind space left to do our job. Furthermore, if our relationship with Bill or Mary really has been harmed, we may have made our job that much harder — all because we wagged our tongue thoughtlessly for one split second.

SOMETIMES YOU NEED TO SPEAK
WHEN YOU DON'T WANT TO.
SOMETIMES YOU NEED NOT
TO SPEAK WHEN YOU DO WANT TO.

TIP 9

Gossip carefully.

Evolutionary psychologists have proposed that office gossip is our contemporary means of fulfilling a genetic need. It is how we come to understand the way "our" group — the group we belong to — expresses itself. We gossip and enjoy listening to gossip because we have a hereditary urge to know what's going on and a similar natural urge to add our observations to the group pool.

It looks like we're hardwired to gossip. Even if that's true, there's still an enormous difference between smiling when you hear that Jim and Helen are jockeying for the corner office versus adding your two cents' worth. Do you really need to add that Jim always seems to be on break and that Helen seems to leave early every day and that neither of them deserves an office with a view?

Adding to office gossip can come back to haunt us. It also doesn't feel very principled.

We feel our smallest, sneakiest, meanest, and cattiest when we gossip. Part of us enjoys it, but another part — the better part — recognizes that we are indulging some primitive urge and not living up to our highest standards. For the same reason, we are inclined to walk away when other people are gossiping. It doesn't feel any better to hear evil than to speak it.

Gossip a little — it's only natural. But gossip carefully, and keep it to a minimum. You are obliged to communicate but you are not obliged to chat idly or maliciously about absent people.

YOUR GENES MAY TELL YOU
TO GOSSIP.
BUT WHAT DOES YOUR BRAIN SAY?

TIP 10

Be clear about
your motivation
before you speak.

Too often we don't understand the impetus behind the things we say. We may think that we are angry about not getting a raise and storm into our supervisor's office to vent. What really may be going on is that we have been looking for a way to leave our job for some time and are taking this opportunity to seal our fate. Or we may think that we have to give our coworker a piece of our mind because she's been dumping her work on us lately. Our true motivation may be envy over the recognition and kudos she got that we are positive she doesn't deserve.

You can do yourself great harm by not knowing what is really motivating your speech. If you are unaware of your actual intentions, you are in grave danger of saying something you will regret and wish you could retract.

Usually we have a glimmer of our real

motivation. We would know why we intend to say the thing we feel compelled to say if only we stopped for a count of ten and asked ourselves the question, "What's going on here?" The instant we ask that question, we enter into fruitful inner dialogue. We give ourselves the chance to identify any covert motivation secretly animating us.

An aware person says things that she means to say. She knows what is motivating her. An unaware person says things that bubble up for unknown reasons and is a pawn to her secret urges. Become free at work by learning to identify the why behind the things you say.

IF YOU DON'T KNOW WHY
YOU ARE SPEAKING,
YOU DON'T KNOW WHAT
YOU ARE SAYING.

BUILDING YOUR NETWORK AS YOU COMMUNICATE

You are talking to John. John mentions Mary, who sounds like someone worth knowing. You can say nothing and miss the chance to network or you can say any of the following:

- "I wonder if you can let Mary know about our monthly newsletter? She might love to subscribe."
- "I wonder if you could invite Mary to our open house next month?"
- "I wonder if you could drop Mary an E-mail and ask her if she'd be willing to chat with me about the business?"
- "I wonder if I can come with you to that

company party at Mary's that you were telling me about?"

- "I wonder if you can let Mary know that we may be looking to hire next month?"
- "I wonder if Mary might be interested in coming in and giving a presentation? What do you think?"
- "I wonder if Mary might like to consult with us? Do you mind if I give her a call and mention your name?"

Don't be afraid of networking or embarrassed to network. Ask carefully, don't push too hard, take "no" for an answer (unless it sounds like "maybe"), and merrily multiply your possibilities and connections by assertively networking.

TIP 11

Watch out — don't be your own worst communication enemy.

What is your personal communication style? Do you start out by apologizing for what you're about to say and finish by apologizing for what you just said? Do you pride yourself on being very direct and honest — which is actually your way of being aggressive and brutal? Do you say things in a convoluted way, so as to keep your thoughts to yourself and avoid being pinned down? These habits, which flow from personality, produce workplace problems at best and cause harm to ourselves or others at worst.

Because our communication style is a reflection of our personality, to change how we communicate we have to change who we are. This is less difficult than it sounds. If we make the effort to speak in a new way — say, without sandwiching what we say between unnecessary apologies — we automatically begin to grow and change.

Take a few minutes right now and try to identify what your communication style says about you as a person. Envision how you would be different if you changed just one unwanted aspect of that style. Then commit to changing.

For example, tell yourself: "I intend to stop apologizing for having opinions. I believe that over time making this change will produce a more self-confident me."

Not knowing our intentions before we speak, using language to wound, hiding behind jargon-filled messages, never speaking because we fear that we are too stupid or unimportant, or saying contradictory things so as to keep everyone happy are some of the ways we put our worst foot forward. Become self-aware and break these bad habits.

THE SECRET TO BETTER COMMUNICATIONS IS PERSONALITY CHANGE. THE SECRET TO PERSONALITY CHANGE IS COMMUNICATING BETTER.

TIP 12

Criticize artfully.

Anytime we have to tell people that they need to do something differently or that they've done something wrong, we are criticizing them. We may hope that we are saying, "You are okay but what you are doing is not okay," but even if we are careful about making that distinction the person receiving our communication is going to feel wounded.

Still, you can do your best to inflict a mere flesh wound or — cruelly and unfairly — you can go for a fatal stab wound. That really is your choice. You can use the moment to vent, to get a dig in, or to let negative feelings about work in general infect the message you are sending. You can let your anger about something else leak into your evaluation. You can publicly ridicule someone, rather than keeping it a private matter. You can make it sound as if the person you're criticizing has never done a commendable thing in her life. In short, you can end up at *more* fault than the person you are criticizing.

Here are some examples of workplace criticism, from worst to best.

PURE VENTING:

"This report is a piece of sh-t! You're an idiot!"

GENTEEL VENTING, WITH A DIG INTENDED:

"You didn't do a very good job on this report. What were you thinking?"

DIRECT CRITICISM, UNADORNED BUT ALSO UNHELPFUL:

"This report doesn't work."

SEPARATING THE PERSON FROM THE PRODUCT AND STARTING WITH A POSITIVE:

"You're usually terrific at this, but this report doesn't work."

SEPARATING THE PERSON FROM THE PRODUCT, STARTING WITH A POSITIVE, AND ALSO PROVIDING HELP:

"You're usually terrific at this, but this report doesn't work. I need you to revise it, especially the last part, where you make your recommendations without telling us why they would be good for us to implement."

Offering artful criticism takes thought and effort, but it pays off in the end. Because of the care you take, there will be fewer ruptures to repair and interpersonal fires to put out.

EVERY NEGATIVE EVALUATION
IS A CRITICISM.
BE MINDFUL OF THE DAMAGE
YOU MIGHT DO BEFORE YOU SPEAK.

CREATE HEADLINE SENTENCES ABOUT YOU AND YOUR WORK

If you want to talk to an audience about your product or service and have them hear you and respond to your message, you must remember that they are human beings with no vested interest in your subject. Their minds are already full of ideas, opinions, and chatter of all sort.

Given this competition, what will make them interested and bring them to your side? Your artful presentation, one rehearsed and crafted, that grips them and stirs their interest. Just as politicians use talking points and salespeople use pitches, you need your own short, sweet, gripping pitch that quickly and effectively piques a listener's interest.

Your pitch can be as short as three strong sentences. One is a sentence about you. The second is a sentence about your business. The third is a sentence about the particular product or service you are offering. For example:

"I've been the marketing v.p. at Really GreatSites.com for the past two years. We specialize in helping freelance Web site designers produce functional Web sites that even our grandparents can use. Our new service is a one-year, no-hidden-costs design consulting package that gives you complete access to our Web-based tools and our human resources with a guaranteed turnaround time of twenty-four hours."

CRAFT YOUR PITCH, MAKING SURE
THAT EVERY WORD COUNTS.

TIP 13

Be generous
with your praise.

People like to be praised. More than that, they *need* praise. It is extremely hard to work month in and month out without anyone recognizing that you are doing a good job or telling you that your contribution is valued. Your performance and your psyche both suffer unless you get positive feedback and an occasional pat on the back.

Praise people at work whenever you can. If you get the chance to give that praise in public, by all means do so. Remember that a simple "thank you" is its own kind of praise. Get in the habit of responding with a heartfelt "thank you" every time you receive something, whether it's a folder or a hot lead, and every time someone does something requiring extra effort, even if it is just remembering to turn off the heat at the end of day.

Giving praise is easier if you feel that your work environment is a positive place. Make it a more positive place by recognizing its good aspects and by checking to discover the small silver lining in every message you receive. Once you train yourself to notice small silver linings — that an employee made a mistake but reported it quickly, that a vendor was late with a delivery but offered a discount on the next order by way of apology — you will always have something ready and waiting to be praised.

PEOPLE NEED TO BE
THANKED AND PRAISED.
PAT PEOPLE ON THE BACK
EVERY CHANCE YOU GET.

TIP 14

Keep people informed — even if it's bad news.

We don't want to burden our fellow workers with unnecessary messages. Nor do we want a mountain of trivial messages coming our way. At the same time, it's crucial that we keep others informed about important news and stay informed ourselves. No part of an organization can work in isolation. We need to know from customer service if we're being deluged with complaints about our latest product, we need to know from marketing that everyone must hurry up if we're going to take advantage of a new sales avenue, and so on.

It is more difficult to keep others informed if the news we need to relay is bad news. Our fantasy is that bad news will go away. It won't. If our department is going to miss a deadline and other departments need to know about it, the longer we put off speaking the more damage we will do to all concerned. It isn't pleasant to have to say that something went wrong, that someone failed, that more work is required, or that people can't have what they were counting on, but we must still find the way — and the courage — to say it.

**BAD NEWS BECOMES WORSE NEWS
IF YOU KEEP IT A SECRET.**

TIP 15

Learn to identify all the information that messages contain.

Consider how the following five messages differ:

1. "Come to my office and we'll chat about the Smith business."
2. "Come to my office and we'll chat about that *damned* Smith business."
3. "Come to my office and we'll chat about that Smith business. Don't forget!"
4. "Come to my office and update me on that Smith business."
5. "Come to my office and I'll let you know what I've decided about that Smith business."

The first makes us feel like an equal. The second announces that the Smith business is a problem. In the third, we're being criticized. The fourth asserts that we have the job of explaining the Smith business. The fifth informs us that the Smith business is out of our hands.

Every time words are put together by a human being, information is conveyed about the sender's intention, attitude, and state of mind. Often this additional information is the most important part of the message. Train yourself to examine the messages you receive for every bit of information they contain.

FIRST, GET THE FACTS STRAIGHT.
THEN READ DEEPLY
BETWEEN THE LINES.

Use the ABC Rule: Be Affirmative, Brief, and Clear

What does being affirmative sound like?

Wrong: "I know that someone with more experience than me might do a better job of setting up our quality assurance system, and I admit that I don't know exactly how it might look...."

Right: "I have been thinking hard about our quality assurance system and I believe that I am exactly the right person to turn it around."

What does being brief sound like?

Wrong: "I had a lot of trouble getting what I wanted to say pared down, so I ended up writing maybe two hundred thousand words to begin with, then I took all those notes up with me to Maine to this cabin that my father-in-law uses for duck hunting, which is not something I condone — duck hunting, that is — but I must admit that the cabin is beautiful...."

RIGHT: "My novel is 75,000 words long."

What does being clear sound like?

WRONG: "I've had the opportunity to connect with forensic details over the past dozen years, both in a lab setting and in the field...."

RIGHT: "I've been a coroner for twelve years."

Practice being affirmative, brief, and clear.

TIP 16

Before you say a big thing, test the waters with mini-messages.

Sometimes the smart thing to do is to float a trial balloon before you shoot up your big rocket. For example:

- You want a certain assignment, but you're not sure how your boss views your current work performance. You might test the waters by saying to her, "I'm interested in taking on a fresh challenge. Do you mind if I keep my eyes open for any new assignments around here?"

- You wish that a certain difficult employee would leave. But you are not in a position to fire him because you have failed to give him regular, adequate evaluations. The road to his release might begin with "John, I need to get on track with my formal evaluations. Let's sit down and do one on Friday." This announcement alone may get him thinking about looking for another job.

- You've been approached to leave your present company. The offer is attractive but you would rather stay where you are, if you were given a raise and a new title. You can't use the job offer as leverage because, if he got wind that you were thinking of leaving, your boss would consider you a traitor and never forgive you. What can you do? There is no perfect course of action in this complex, difficult situation. But the alternatives to floating a trial balloon — namely being direct or saying nothing — have their own significant drawbacks. Circumspectly testing the waters may prove to be the most reasonable course of action.

WHAT YOU SAY IS UP TO YOU.
IT COULD BE A BOMBSHELL OR
SOMETHING ARTFUL AND CUNNING.

TIP 17

Practice empathy.

Empathy is the ability to understand another person's thoughts and feelings. It is the mind-reading, feeling-reading ability built into each one of us, yet many of us have trouble accessing this amazing skill. What about you? Can you enter another person's world at the drop of a hat, whenever and with whomever you converse? Do your listening skills, life experiences, and intuitions about human nature come together and help you read people? Could any skill be more valuable in the workplace?

Sometimes, when we empathize with someone, we begin to care about him or her and feel sympathy and compassion. But empathy is first and foremost a survival skill. The more adept you become at reading people, at sensing instantly what they're thinking and feeling, the better equipped you become at knowing what messages to send and how to frame them. If you can let down your defenses, quiet the chatter in your mind, and turn all your attention to the person opposite you, you will suddenly know what her words and actions mean.

Your boss may say that she can't act on your latest idea. Because you empathize with her, realize that she had to run your idea by her supervisor, and read something in her body language and hesitant presentation, you would know what to reply. "I wonder," you might say, "is the 'no' coming from you or from Jack?"

This may give her the opening she needs to say, "Yes, Jack's the one who doesn't care for it! I don't agree with him. I wish we could find another angle."

Working together, you can brainstorm

ways to reframe your idea. The chance to resuscitate your idea came about solely because you practiced empathy.

IF YOU COMMUNICATE DEFENSIVELY,
RATHER THAN EMPATHICALLY,
PEOPLE WILL REMAIN
A LIFELONG MYSTERY TO YOU.

IF YOU WANT SOMETHING, FIRST PREPARE YOUR CASE

Do you want that vacant corner office? The chance to manage that big project? That overseas assignment? To get it, you know that you will have to speak. But before you speak, prepare your case.

For example:

- "I know that the budget is tight, but I would love to attend two conferences next year, both the national and the international. Let me tell you why I think this is not only justified but a really good idea. . . ."

- "I know that we've pretty much decided what to put on our next album. But I have a new song that I'd like us to consider including. I think it would work beautifully as the third song. Remember, we were already thinking that something different should go there...."

- "I know that you're considering me for Dave's old job. But I think I should step all the way up to the spot Sally vacated. There are three excellent reasons why I'm the right person for that job...."

- "I would like to have a sabbatical next year. I know it's the policy not to give one until a person has been here seven years, but I think there are compelling reasons for making an exception in my case...."

When you want something, spend real time preparing your case.

Then muster your courage and present it!

TIP 18

Learn to say what
your job demands
that you say.

Some of the things that we have to say at work can make us feel extremely uncomfortable. We may have to deny a person a loan, advocate for a client we don't like, tell a mother that her child is gravely ill, break a deal because of changing circumstances, withhold the truth as a matter of company policy, refuse service when a person can't pay, or sing the praises of a product we don't believe in. We may have to reprimand and fire. We may have to issue life-and-death orders. Our work life comes with duties, responsibilities, and — invariably — a shadow side. When we put on our work clothes we agree to abide by the rules of our chosen game, even when the rules make us feel sad or guilty.

If we want to live an activist life, we can fight to change the rules we particularly dislike. If our dislike grows too great, we can leave. But the truth is that every workplace puts words in our mouth. We can't be a lawyer, doctor, priest, counselor, salesperson, cop, editor, waiter, or anything under the sun without being forced to say things like "Have a nice day!" or "Get your hands up!" Every job demands that, for some portion of the time, we stifle what we wish we could say and opt for what we *must* say.

GET USED TO YOUR
PROFESSIONAL LANGUAGE.
IT MAY NOT FEEL NATURAL,
BUT — READY OR NOT — IT'S
YOURS NOW.

TIP 19

Grow as a
communicator by
stretching and risking.

Maybe you find it easy to express your feelings but hard to issue orders. Maybe you can cold call without breaking a sweat but never share your opinions in meetings. Maybe you listen well to what your friends have to say but listen less patiently at work. Each of us has strengths and weaknesses when it comes to communicating: Do you know yours?

Have you ever stopped to identify your own communication strengths and weaknesses? Give it a try right now. It won't take you more than a few minutes. Just get a sheet of paper, draw a line down the middle, label one column "strengths" and the other column "weaknesses," and be honest with yourself.

Congratulate yourself on your strengths. Then take a look at the other column. Probably everything there feels important. Still, try to single out one weakness that you feel is particularly crucial to overcome. Maybe this is your fear of stating your opinions. Maybe it is the brutal way you present your ideas. Maybe it is your inability to really listen. Circle the most important one. Focus on it. Try to think of one small step you could take that would move you in the direction of change. Envision taking that step. Can you picture yourself doing it?

Tell yourself when and where you will actually take that first baby step. "At tomorrow's planning meeting I am going to stand up and state my opinions." "When Jennifer comes in today, I am going to stop myself from hitting her over the head with my ideas." "The next person who calls, no matter what the call is about, I am going to give that person my undivided attention."

Envision the step, rehearse it in your mind, and then *do it*.

BECOME AN EXCELLENT COMMUNICATOR. YOUR CAREER DEPENDS ON IT.

TIP 20

Always speak in a principled way.

It's not too principled to avoid thinking a policy through and then demanding that others act on your unclear instructions. It's not too principled to refuse to consider the consequences of what you're proposing. It's not too principled to treat others as inferior, just because you hold the power. It's not too principled to think that you are the only one with an investment in the decisions that affect you. We abide by our own good principles at work — or we don't and fail ourselves.

How we communicate is a function of what we are thinking and feeling, how we view others, and what principles we have chosen to champion. I may claim to believe that rudeness is unjustified, but if I am rude when I speak then I am articulating my *actual* life principle. If I demean and belittle people when I speak, I am displaying my insides and announcing, "This is how I *really* view life."

"Speak in a principled way" is just a variation of the Golden Rule. Do you want to be included? Include others. Do you want to be treated as a full partner? Treat others as full partners, too. Do you want people to speak to you so meekly and indirectly that you never know what they are saying? If you don't, then model strong, direct speech. Do you want to be patronized or ridiculed by those above you? If you don't, keep that principle in mind when you speak to those below you.

It isn't in your power to transform your company into a principled workplace. But you do have the power to model principled speaking and listening. You do have the power to communicate clearly and directly. You do have the power to articulate your values by what you say, what you refrain from saying, how you listen, and how you respond. Your values will even peek through by the way you say "Hello" and "How are you?" Remember: You are what you say.

WHAT YOU SAY REFLECTS WHO YOU ARE. WHO DO YOU WANT TO BE?

How to Ask for What You Want

As with all communication in any relationship, there are right ways and wrong ways to ask for something. The best reason to use the right way is that it usually gets the best results.

WRONG: "Charlie is driving me crazy! I need him to straighten up!"

RIGHT: "I need Charlie to come in on time every day and not leave before five."

WRONG: "I need a better effort from you."

RIGHT: "I need you to handle some routine matters, like checking orders and processing requests, that you've been passing on to me. I believe that you can take the initiative on those."

Wrong: "I need some help!"

Right: "I need a half-time assistant to handle the billing and the filing, so I can work on upgrading our computer system."

Wrong: "Cut down on the #$%^%$# noise in here!"

Right: "We have to limit the personal visits of people from other departments."

Wrong: "I'm having so many day-care problems!"

Right: "I support the idea of an on-site day-care facility."

Wrong: "Read my mind and give me what I want!"

Right: "This is what I want...."

Afterword

The workplace is the epitome of the real world. What we say to customers, clients, coworkers, supervisors, and every single person we come into contact with not only has the potential to help us or harm us, but it actually does help us or harm us. One angry, impulsive message can ruin an important business relationship. One carefully prepared, well-delivered message can get us a better job or land us a big order. How we communicate at work profoundly affects the job we do and the trajectory of our career.

Become a skilled communicator. This means unlearning bad habits, letting go of rules against speaking that may have been imposed in your family, growing so self-aware that you know how your personality affects what you say, learning new communication skills, and taking the time to practice them. This requires real effort, but the rewards are tremendous. Not only will you transform yourself into a more effective and valued professional, but you will dramatically increase your self-confidence. Try out these twenty tips and see the difference they make — at work, and in the rest of your life, too!

8413

Eric Maisel, Ph.D., is a licensed marriage and family therapist and a management lecturer at St. Mary's College (Moraga, California). He is a nationally known creativity consultant whose books include *The Creativity Book, Fearless Creating, A Life in the Arts, Deep Writing, Affirmations for Artists, Fearless Presenting,* and *Living the Writer's Life.* This is Dr. Maisel's second volume in New World Library's 20 Tips series; his first, *20 Communication Tips for Families,* appeared in 2000. He is also the author of novels and other nonfiction, including the recently published *Sleep Thinking.*

Dr. Maisel lives in Concord, California, with his wife Ann Mathesius Maisel, associate head of San Francisco's Lick-Wilmerding High School, and their younger daughter, Kira, a junior in high school. Their elder daughter, Natalya, is a student at the University of California at Berkeley, and Dr. Maisel's son by his first marriage, David, lives in Amsterdam, where he works in cyberspace and flies small planes in actual space. The Maisels also have four cats: Max, Sam, Charlie, and Bailey.

Dr. Maisel is available to speak about effective communicating at work. He would also love to hear your thoughts and feelings about this book and about your communication successes and challenges on the job. He can be reached in the following ways: